Gold Star Road

Winner of the Barrow Street Press Poetry Prize,
selected by Molly Peacock

Gold Star Road

Richard Hoffman

Barrow Street Press
New York City

Designed by Robert Drummond ·

Cover photo: Carol Guzy

Published by Barrow Street Press
Distributed by:
       Barrow Street
       P.O. Box 1831
       Murray Hill Station
       New York, NY 10156

First Edition

Library of Congress control number: 2007904508

ISBN 978-0-9728-302-7-0 (Softcover)
ISBN 978-0-9728302-8-7 (Hardcover)

for Kathi

CONTENTS

Headache Clinic

tortures are just what they were, only the earth has shrunk
and whatever goes on sounds as if it's just a room away.
                    —Wisława Szymborska

Yes, the pain is worse since last time I was here;
I've tried to become accustomed to it. Last night
while I was trying to find a comfortable position
and wondering if I should take a pill,
a man a couple of miles from here came home,
walked quietly upstairs, took out his gun,
and murdered his wife and two children,
a boy and a girl, while they slept.
The paper had photos. He shot himself too.
A fourteen-year-old's parents want to know
who duct-taped the bombs to his hairless chest
under the Warner Bros. T-shirt his uncle
brought him with a cap from Florida last year.
Doctor, when you shine that penlight in my eyes,
do you see the man take off his shoes inside the door
so as not to wake his sleeping wife and kids?
You want me to point to the part of my head that hurts?
That's it, that part. I can follow your finger, yes,
from where the boy left the small repair garage,
past the tented bookstall and the cashew vendors,
to where he entered the crowded restaurant.
Do you see her? The woman, her finger in the air,
who has just caught the eye of the waiter?
On a scale of 1 to 10, your pen in hand, you ask,
"How badly does it hurt right now?"

Bosnia Aftermath

for Sara Terry

A trout on a riverbank
knows where the river is;

a fox in a trap
knows the time,

but a man or woman
only knows the story

hope tells, or fear,
and often chooses wrong.

No ant will enter
another's hill,

no bee another's hive,
and a rook, atop

a dead oak,
knows which side it's on,

but a man or woman,
led by liars,

will discuss, calmly,
who should dig the pit

and if it is a better
lesson to slaughter

the neighbors' babies
first or afterward.

A squirrel burrows deep
in a hollow trunk;

the bear returns
to her darkened cave,

but a man or woman,
gorged on blood,

deep in history, asleep,
dreams peace

and waking, says
peace is a dream.

A rabbit may cower,
but only so long;

the common sparrow
knows the seasons,

but a man or woman
only wants a song, a poem,

a religion to profess
that no one who has known

goodness even once
is ever wholly lost.

Refugee

A man carries his door,
the door of his house,
because when the war is over
he is going home

where he will hang it
on its hinges
and lock it, tight,
while he tries to remember
the word for welcome.

If his house is gone
when he returns,
he will raise it from rubble
around this door.

If he cannot return,
the door will remember
the rest of the house
so he can build it
again, elsewhere.

And if he cannot go on,
his door can be a pallet
for his rest, a stretcher
to carry him, his shade
from sun, his shield.

Without Wings

for Swanee Hunt

In the cemetery, angels,
women of stone, read
books of what is done
and cannot be changed.
Not far away, women
are carrying handbags,
as if shopping, along rows
of unearthed remains
in the high school gym.
They have hurried past
the empty pedestal
in the sniper's sights,
crawled from blasted buses,
lied, dissembled, hidden
the fugitive, given
the refugee a warm
loaf for the journey,
slipped past checkpoints
and remembered
where each tree, gate,
garden used to be,
and in which books
the words are written
that tell, despite what
has been done, what
must be done.

The Judgment of Paris

An apple,
three questioning looks;

six nipples,
a flood of want, one choice

among graces,
put to the usual uses

by generals: havoc
in a great wave washing over us.

Gold Star Road

Tragedies begin with messengers
so we were fooled: we watched
the sea and sky, hoping
to see nothing strange. Ignorant

as goldfish in a plastic bag,
as mayflies mistaking the road for the river,
we assured one another,

keeping up our spirits
as we had long been taught.

*

We lived in a white cosmopolis.
Domes, temples, obelisks, and plazas
spoke suggestions. Landscapes,
in their changing light, concurred.
Now it is as if we have taken shelter
in darkness under a bridge.
Whose steps do we hear above us?
Whose wheels rumble the roadbed?
Who casts this shadow even here in the dark
we feel pass over us like shame?

*

Half in, half out of dream, I could not wake.
I stumbled when I tried to stand.
I have known the whole night long how many
will insist, to stave off ridicule,
that the words they find on their lips are their own.
Three or four congruent lies define a view
even fact, even fear, even love
can't change. The killers, the dead, the grieving,
I have seen the whole night long their faces.

*

Not in uniform, three-quarters profile,
chinstrapped, scowling, a flag behind, but

with a dog, or polishing a hubcap,
big boy picking up his laughing mother.

When we say we will remember
what we mean is we will learn

to translate flesh to colored inks,
grief to convention. Should their names

come up in conversation we will have these
in a drawer to conjure them again, and

tell ourselves we have what fate allowed.
Often we cannot bring their bodies home.

*

The streetlamp outside my bedroom window,
I have seen it thousands of nights.
In summer, moths; in winter, snow
turns, in its cone of light, to angled sleet.
At its foot the children gather, play late.
Good guys and bad guys. Bang, you're dead.

What a small life. What good dreams
for so long. Now we understand
that this was never really peace, that
this neighborhood, this soft light, even
these children were never ours, and
even their play did not belong to them.

*

Horrible to say so, but
memory, like a flat rock, skims
and skips: once — twice —

before it splashes the purplish
waters, wobbles
irrevocably
bottomward, and

clicks there against the smooth
thoughts of the emptied dead.

*

Our enemies proved their superior
brutality by torturing their children,

starving them, refusing them medicine,
raising them in ignorance and executing

them for crimes they could not understand.
We had no choice. We would have lost

had we not followed suit. We regret
all of it, but our walls still stand.

*

A bright light in a doorway spoke:
To wake you must remember this dream.
Though I had already forgotten,
I promised and passed through the door.

The sun is up and the newspaper lies,
folded, on the top step. My neighbor
waves, already sweeping the sidewalk.
They are kind, the people where I live.

Some modified inherited disguises;
some, like going to a new barber,
chose from pictures in a book;
some shed their fictions and saw there,

under the pillar's chipped plaster,
chicken wire. Most begged: *Please
give us something to say we believe
so we can go on about our business.*

Caesar

Arriving at the podium on the tarmac,
he stands up tall and makes a big fuss
rolling up his sleeves like drawing back

his foreskin, and only amnesiacs
still traumatized and children
do not know what happens next.

Broadcast

The one-legged man in the caftan said,
in his own tongue, that after the war,
the armies left their landmines in the fields.
The translator told the camera that the
enemy, retreating, had mined the roads.

"I know who is responsible for this,"
the man said in his native language, but
the correspondent asked him how he felt
when chosen for a new titanium limb.
"If you don't mind, we'd like," the camera-
man said, "a close-up, please, of your injury."

The man hiked up his robe and said,
in his own tongue, of course, "I speak
for many others. I can sometimes feel
the dead the way I sometimes feel my leg.
Our home is poisoned, famine spreads, the children
starved or sold to pedophiles in Europe.
There are no books, no music, no one who
can read or play or plan." The interpreter
reported that the man was very grateful.

A car pulled up, the rear door opened, and
the correspondent introduced the man
who'd paid for the victim's trip here, for his care,
and for his state-of-the-art prosthesis.

"You are the one!" said the one-legged man,
"the generals gave, for money to Swiss accounts,
the mineral rights to my country!" But they ran
old footage then of hobbling children, spoke
of the generous man's campaign to clear the fields.
A number to call flashed on the screen. Up next:
The rising price of crude. We'll be right back.

An Emblem from Dresden

In Rembrandt's *The Rape of Ganymede*[1]
    the boy, a chubby toddler torn from his play,
        kicks and wails and pisses in terror as,

clamped in beak and talon, he looks down.
    The sky is smoke, a billowing smudge
        as after the bombardment of a city.

The eagle is unnatural, painted in the way
    myth borrows nature for its purposes,
        larger and more saurian, power from on high,

but the boy, as Rembrandt understood, is real
    and not especially beautiful, a fat boy fed
        the diet of the poor: potatoes, turnips, bread,

and for sweetness the cherries in his fist.
    Ovid has Orpheus sing the story Hermes,
        the slippery consigliere, tells the parents:

the boy will learn the language of the mighty,
    an acolyte, loved and provided for, a story
        that comes with a payment of valuable horses,

wealth enough to secure the future, more
    than even a grown son could expect to earn
        them. What does the boy see, rising? Over Laos

200,000 children trafficked into Thailand's
    brothels, building sites, and sweatshops; over
        Kazahkstan, Uzbekistan, Afghanistan, Albania,

procurers riding shotgun, helicopter cargo
    bound for prostitution in the streets of Athens;
        from Nigeria, bush pilots make the short flight

over jungle to the secret auction, "Clean, no HIV. No HIV."
      Euros for their trouble from the French, the Belgians;
            dollars from Americans.[2] The eagle on the money,

each child a disappearance. "Too young," says the madam,
      pulling back the beaded curtain for her client,
            "no boom-boom this one, not yet, only yum-yum."

---

[1] 1635, oil on canvas, 171 x 130 cm, Gemäldegalerie, Dresden.
[2] US Dept of State, Human Rights Report, 1999; ECPAT International, "A Step Forward,"
1999; and UNICEF, "State of the World's Children," 1997.

Humanities 101, an Essay

First day I give out the syllabus,
tell them what I have planned,
and that the readings will address
individual freedom on the one hand

and responsibility on the other.
A couple of them look interested;
the others inspect one another.
One asks how they'll be tested.

Or, I wonder, how will I? Each
time I stand here, scared, every fall,
I ask myself what I have to teach
these novices; who am I after all

but another who inclined toward
convention and away from injury,
who hid in the crowd, a coward?
Crowd/coward: rhyme of the century,

the last one, that is — almost *in fact*
the last one, when The End of History
was declared by those who in effect
were writing it and (hiding in theory,

their conceptual Trojan horse)
saddling this generation, like mine,
with another of their filthy wars.
I feel inadequate and asinine,

like some dried-out whiskey priest
remorseful and trying to make
of his pocked and broken life at least
a bold, exemplary mistake.

Yet Icarus, the moth-boy, with neither
chart nor fear, with a surfeit of strength
but no sense, has begun to feather
the great wings' width and length

with perfect, long, gray goosequills
sitting in the back of the class,
and Antigone, by wireless e-mail, tells
her Uncle Creon he can kiss her ass

so that once again, as in the fables,
rebellion's back on top of evil
as the tilted planet turns the tables,
making the tyrant sun-god shrivel,

dunked again in the daily water,
nothing now but a picture postcard
an errant son or zealous daughter
might send home. Or homeward

anyway, to where their parents,
with their new, corrective spouses,
hope to rediscover innocence
individually, in separate houses

in a century in which we all are free
to believe we can begin again
so long as we behave responsibly
by watching the world on Fox or CNN.

Group Portrait

Around the table men are waiting
for their president to arrive.
They are like hard cases for instruments —
plush inside, with clever compartments
for reed or mute, mouthpiece or bow,

but when the doors swing open and the chief
strides in, a thrill goes through them all
like children in the back of a schoolbus
when you wave at them or toot your horn
so that they have to remind themselves

this is serious: today they are discussing
the best date to begin the war and which
of several possible cities to bombard.
The lights are dimmed; a screen rolls down.
They settle deeper in the dark, adjust themselves.

A Bronze Star for Ssgt. Camilo Mejia[3]

When, in the face of the enemy, conscience,
all the others fled,
when the generals shrank from empathy
and, challenged to commiserate, officers turned tail,

Camilo did not run.

When it was clear that unless they took to their heels,
understanding and remorse
would easily outflank and overtake them,

Camilo did not run.

When multiple battalions,
staring down the barrel of fellow-feeling,
stampeded like a frightened herd,

when the commander-in-chief,
confronted with pity, deserted,
along with his circle of ministers
and hid in the country of rhetoric,
deep in the bunker of ideology,

Camilo stood his ground

3 Ssgt. Camilo Mejia was the first active duty soldier in the Iraq War to file for
Conscientious Objector status. On refusing to return to Iraq, he was court-
martialed and found guilty of desertion.

Blog Pix: Fallujah

I call it cruel and maybe the root of all cruelty
to know what occurs but not recognize the fact.
—William Stafford

Far away in Fallujah,
flies lift off from piled corpses,
wheel like sparrows over
stubbled fields or
shorebirds at ebbtide

in formation, dark then light
then dark, alighting
again, in unison, a black mesh
veiling faces and milky eyes.

But I wasn't there in Fallujah,
I only saw photographs
of the flies in Fallujah;

perhaps the flies of Fallujah
behave differently from other flies.

*

A frightened soldier in Fallujah
shot an unarmed captive in the head.
I saw it on the Internet.

You cannot trust the Internet.
Unlike the news on TV,
no one controls what's on the Internet.

But I wasn't there in Fallujah.
Perhaps frightened soldiers in Fallujah
behave differently from frightened soldiers elsewhere.

*

A child with one leg
bleeds on a mattress in Fallujah,
disposable diaper for a bandage.

But this could be staged,
doctored.

Perhaps bombs in Fallujah
behave differently from other bombs.

*

A man leans his head
against the wooden coffin on his shoulder
and weeps in the streets of Fallujah;

his eyes are shut tight;
there is blood on his brow.
His comrade? His sister? His mother? His child?

I was not there in the streets of Fallujah
and there is no caption.
There is no one I love far away in Fallujah.

Perhaps in Fallujah grief
has only sadness in it;
no rage, no desire for vengeance.

Perhaps grief in Fallujah
is different from grief in other places.

School: A Memoir

There was a child went forth every day;
And the first object he look'd upon, that object he became;
And that object became part of him for the day, or a certain part of
the day, or for many years, or stretching cycles of years.

—Walt Whitman

i. A candle

Even before I was taught
to burn, I dreamed
of a greater darkness,

and every time I was
extinguished (a thumb
on my throat, a face
coming close)

I fell back into
that fragrant memory,

no longer the center of night,
no longer knowing myself
diminishing.

ii. A book

All the pictures folded in the dark
inside me — people, animals, roads,
the mailman bringing news from far away,
machinery, saints, and mountains —
were illustrations to a story
children who took me home
tried hard to learn to read.

iii. A kiss

Poor coat hangers,
standard
wire, without
even paper sleeves, yet

in the schoolroom closet
when we touched,
we rang!

iv. A pencil

The point is lost
again and again

and trying only
makes me smaller,

broken as I am
inside.

v. The corner

Two walls meet here
or stretch away from each other
or both — like a book

where, shamed,
I
mark the place

— or wings,
mine, to fly
from those with the answers.

Summer Job

"The trouble with intellectuals," Manny, my boss,
once told me, "is that they don't know nothing
till they can explain it to themselves. A guy like that,"
he said, "he gets to middle age — and by the way,
he gets there late; he's trying to be a boy until
he's forty, forty-five, and then you give him five
more years until that craziness peters out, and now
he's almost fifty — a guy like that at last explains
to himself that life is made of time, that time
is what it's all about. Aha! he says. And then
he either blows his brains out, gets religion,
or settles down to some major-league depression.
Make yourself useful. Hand me that three-eighths
torque wrench — no, you moron, the other one."

Doorman

Bright buttons, white gloves, polished shoes,
I kept the glass clean and the brass knobs shining.
A captain's hat and trousers creased and striped,
some tatting on the sleeves, a touch of braid.
It might have been a soldier's uniform.

Over and over, day after day, I opened
the same door for the same rich people
who pretended to think we were equals,
while I, who needed the job to pay rent,
pretended to believe they thought so.

I was so bored it made me happy
to run into the street and blow my little whistle
then stand there holding the door of a cab
as if I'd just caught a great big fish!
Even if what I do now doesn't matter

as much as I want to think it does, even if
I'm a fool in other ways than I was back then,
I never want to do that kind of work again:
over and over, day after day, opening
the same door for the same rich people.

Vocation

Because I was born into ongoing falsehood,
I have had to learn to think in metaphors,
to lash together what could be found on
each small island of that barren archipelago,

to learn what would float, to find what would
carry me. It is only when I am tired I pity the
various people I have been or, worse, deny them.
I have not met anyone who is entirely who

he thinks he is, nor people anywhere so strange
they did not, somehow, move me. When death comes
I have left instructions for my friends to put me
back in the thesaurus with my ancestors.

Psalm

I honor the newt who grows back his crushed tail
and mourn the time lost to that healing.
I am sorry not to have kept to the path.

I celebrate the trout at the bottom of the lake
in the icy slush where he doesn't even shiver,
and wish the dead would pick up after themselves.

I applaud the living cuckoo who,
unlike his wooden cousin, does not keep time,
and regret that I have not yet climbed the mountain.

Cranes fly over Everest three miles up!
I recall at least one afternoon that lasted years.
I apologize for having been away so long.

Runt

The others, full,
each with his myth,
lay curled in explanation's
dreamless sleep

while you,
the final drop
from each dug yours,
imbibed desire,

its edge, its many
tastes, its uses
and power, its fine
unrealizable
idea of satiety, and

imagined paradise
where the forbidden
cracked
when you bit it,
and the juice
rolled down your chin.

Blackbird

One descends from the tall pines, first
simply falling a moment before the opening
of wings and then the long glide over

the marsh to land on a chosen cattail (chosen
when? at what point before or during the flight?)
that rocks as the wings are folded and the song

begins, more checks and whistles than warbling,
no awards here for eloquent phrasing or variety.
It doesn't sing about its flying, it just flies.

Riverbank

The water-combed otter
does not know its name
because both are syllables
in the river's poem

no wonder some
say were I ash
I could be part of that
instead of this

but then I could not
see the way
sun on the water
reflected on this tree

resembles fire, nor
wonder and look
at minnows, merely
sparks, more

motion than flesh,
or hear geese
honk excitement
leaving. Death,

you can't have me,
I belong here
among these creatures
and their practical joy.

First Weekend in September

Already it's late summer. Look!
That fat bee fumbling on a thistle,
that gray squirrel's spiral up the oak,
that grackle in tattered silks,
that retriever in the shade, panting;

white pine, red pine, spruce the color
of the breath on blueberries, people
with looks on their faces, in their lives,
a brown trout fanning in a shallow pool
so clear the waterbugs have shadows!

Some days I think I understand
how it can be that in all of this
there are no minor lives. Not one
speck anywhere that doesn't cry out
"Spare me!" Then my own despair,

my own choked cry: will even my
wonder not survive? Even my revulsion
at the curled and stiffened pickerel
floating belly-up, discolored, in the weeds?
All I can do is look harder.

Cove

Small waves repeat,
disappear on sand,
stairs of an escalator

down. I forgot what
I meant to say. I forgot
what I meant to say.

Soft flesh in a broken
shell. Tangled rope.
Stones worn human.

To S.

Your friends are worried. Me too.
None of us is certain what to do.
Yesterday your old school roommate
stammered long-distance his belief:
"Advice is useless to a broken heart."
What did he want such country-western
horse manure to do? Excuse our silence?
Elevate you to romantic, tragic hero?
I uh-huhed him then but now I disagree:
With all the sympathy I have I have
to tell you grief excuses nothing.
Make it your friend and it will buy you
all the drinks you want and quite a few
you won't. We would rather not be
loved at all than hurt like this we
think, but soon we would rather not
love either. Pour another. Years
pass. This is why, I think, in bars,
you have to raise your eyes to see
the clock above the mirror. One day
each of us will need whatever love
of sweet oblivion we've learned
from hurt, but this is not that time.
Still, who am I — old fart, old fool —
to tell you how to mourn? Forgive
my gall, and if you ever need to, call.

Airfare

In an airport, I met a man I knew
when we were young. In those days
he was loud, gregarious, intrepid;
I was shy and certain I was stupid,
and I wanted to be more like him.
We made brittle conversation,
and did not exchange addresses.
I did not tell him what he'd been to me.
Later, belted in beside a young child
with her mother seated on the aisle,
I wondered at how we change,
inhibit, and inhabit one another:
friends, enemies, teachers, lovers,
neighbors, students. Even the man
who worked beside me years ago,
both of us soldering circuitboards,
(I think his name was John)
shows up in my dreams sometimes
though he still doesn't say anything.
Feeling as if my life were only mine
the way my seat, 11E, was mine, I
was trying to find, through layers
of scratched Plexiglas and drifting
clouds, a sign of where we were
and how much farther we had to go
when the restless child knocked on my
leg. "Tell me the story. This one,"
and she offered me the trifold card,
wordless but clear to any grown-up,
the one in reassuring pastel colors
where the people lift the cushions,
maybe to look for pennies there.
And here they are on the inflatable
slide, see? Or bobbing in the gentle
waves — without their bathing suits!
I didn't know what else to tell her

so I took my pen from my pocket,
drew some birds in the air, a beach
with some people and a dog on it,
and farther back, a tree. "Now me!"
she said. I gave her the pen; she
bit her tongue and drew and drew.

Here Goes

for Rick Wile

It's time for me to dance
one of the necessary dances
again, the wet dog, maybe,
(stand back!) or the one
I call the suffering snake,
where I take off my clothes
and, naked, kick them
at the gathering circle
of the curious, the difficult
dance that says yes,
I'm naked, but no,
I'm not crazy. Can you
not make the distinction?
Have you forgotten
certain necessary dances
require this sloughing,
this touching earth and air?
Can you not see this is grief?

Pantoum: But You Are Gone

i.m. Robert James Hoffman 1950–1972

I thought for a long time
if I was very quiet
for a long time
I might recall your voice.

If I was very quiet
I might long for you so long
I might recall your voice
as if my ear could sift the wind.

I might long for you so long,
for words you had spoken,
as if my ear could sift the wind
for things you said,

for words you had spoken,
that if I searched my memory
for things you said,
I might find you again;

that if I searched my memory
for a long time,
I might find you again
I thought for a long time.

Chesterfield®

i.m. Dolly Virginia Mattes Hoffman, 1929-1984

Sweat-soaked, a few more moment's worth of breath
fought for and won, begged for and granted, you lay back,
relaxed your grip on my hand and made some crack
about how death had scared you half to death
that time and could you have the cool cloth
on your brow, some ice-chips, please, and your black
St. Joseph's Missal? Nobody's fool, the lack
of any hope moved you to reach for faith.
What else could you, or any of us, do?
Three packs a day for years your balm for grief.
(Dad asked me if I thought that he should sue,
as if the law could bring him back his wife.)
I watched you suffer till your death was proof
oblivion is paradise enough.

December

I love days
like this, alone,
the one clock
in the front hall
counting
peace, peace, peace.
I can hear
snow ticking
on the windows,
now and then a
crumbling on the roof,
and outside,
stumbling through drifts,
someone
calling my name.

Miracle at Bethany

Why? asked Lazarus.
Why come forth?
Is there peace? Are we now
in the time of justice?

I dream of these things
in the dark, in the earth.
It is my work, brother.
Leave me to it.

Déjà Vu

As if a bird
alighted
on a mirror
a moment
and then was gone

(the name

"vireo"

arising
as the image
of the bird
rose
to the bird
but
more slowly)

so, from deep,

grief

is known
afterward,

when even a single
instant
matches it.

Ars

Yes, but
the hammer
was made for the nail,

the plane to shave,
the chisel to hew,

and the drill although
in any gauge
exquisite
is not curled to please.

To an Embryonic Stem Cell

Alphabet. Mockingbird. Skeleton key.
Stoical, stock-still, sharp-eyed lifeguard.
"With no desire or hatred in your heart,
there is no need to show off or pretend."[4]
Soul of generosity, how do you do
it, follow the oftentimes ambiguous,
occasionally erring path the body's
syntax ought to have, among a clutch
of inborn or environmental
choices, made, hone in, and find
where meaning failed, that break,
and fix it? Blank stare, I can see you
there on the bench in the bullpen,
cap pulled down, not signing autographs,
smelling like a brand-new box of crayons,
neat as a shrink-wrapped deck of cards.
Sworn friend. Trickster. Tikkun's angel.
Oblate. Virtuoso. Smooth-cheeked Virgo.
Shaman. Seamus. Speck of spirit.
Eligible, agreeable, truest love.
Divulge your secrets, phoenix fire!
O protein protean and pluripotent,
teach us how to mend our selfish lives.

4 Milarepa, "The Ten Thousand Songs."

Humility

Half a life to open
one gummed eye,

and now I need one hand
to shield it from the light.

And I should say what I
believe I see with certainty?

Vanitas

Consider the carrot:
note, in its skin,
its knuckled
story, scuffed and
scarred, bent
by dry rock, twisted
toward water;
hear, from its look
(as if you could listen
the length
of its time) the rasp
and crunch of its
augur in earth, its
labor on behalf
of its green crown's
sunlit, delicate,
windblown glory
we throw away.

Woodcut Parable, 15th C.[5]

The goddess leads men with twisted ribbons
stronger than chains; her retinue includes a boy,

blindfolded, with a toy-like bow and quiver.
She is led by a humble donkey through the streets,

and where the donkey goes a monkey follows.
A tonsured old drooling monk cannot recall

when last he heard the bell in the tower or
when she first fastened this band to his wrist,

and the fool, likewise bound, for all his antics,
fights back bitter tears the whole way into town,

remembering the day he arrived to woo her,
fresh from running and winning a race, how

when she spread her magnificent wings,
he never saw the death's head leering there

that he sees so clearly now. The donkey brays,
and the monkey, never not looking for something,

is interested in each successive thing until he isn't.
They are on the road. Word has them headed here.

---

5 Albrecht Durer, 1492. Plate XIII ("Of Wooing") in "Das Narrenschift" ("Ship of
Fools") by Sebastian Brant, 1494.

Terms of Occupancy

In heaven you must promise
never to forget
you are in heaven.

In hell you must promise
never to forget
to want to be elsewhere.

On earth you must promise
never to forget
there are no promises.

A Unit Deploys

after Tu Fu's "Ballad of the Army Carts"

Yellow schoolbuses idle at the curb, exhaust rising in the cold from shuddering tailpipes. The soldiers' gear is lined up on the lawn outside the armory. Inside, where the families are gathered, you can hardly hear a thing for the brass band and the pipers playing patriotic music. People are weeping, parents, wives, children, dabbing at their eyes with shredded tissues; some have faces like welts with eyes, while others look disoriented, dazed. The soldiers, boots as black as onyx, names in black on canvas strips above their hearts, wear a strange new kind of camo, all gray angles, for an urban setting.

On a signal they move outside, each retrieving his gear from where he'd left it on the grass, and board the bus like a hockey team off to a tournament. Their families follow them outside, small children hoisted onto shoulders. Some still hurry back and forth to see which bus will carry their loved one away. Then the driver of the first bus in the row grinds the gears and thunks it into first, and the sound of it sets off renewed, involuntary, stifled crying among the families as they wave at the buses pulling away, one after the other, in an orderly convoy.

Gift

My father gave me a small globe,
"This is the world," he said,
and showed me where to put the money.

"Good boy," he said.
"Good-bye! Good luck!"

A lot of good
that did me.

Or him.

I lift and shake it: empty.
It doesn't spin;
it never did,
and the countries are different.

Founders' Gallery

This old man, he play one,
he play walk like I walk, son.
With a six-pack, heart attack,
leave me all alone,
this old man come rolling home.

This old man, he play two,
he play listen I know you.
With a backslap, wisecrack,
cut me to the bone,
this old man drove me from home.

This old man, he play three,
he play don't talk back to me.
With an Abraham and Isaac,
change to baritone,
this old man afflict his home.

This old man, he play four,
he play imitation lore.
With a gimcrack, bronze plaque,
soldier's tomb unknown,
this old man forgot his home.

This old man, he play five,
he play let's see you survive.
With a headwhack, flashback,
man-made danger zone,
this old man oppress his home.

This old man, he play six,
he play world is made of pricks.
With a greenback, smokestack,
no one else can own,
this old man he sold my home.

This old man, he play seven,
he play eight by tens of heaven.
With a Kodak, Cadillac,
turkey's dry wishbone,
this old man lured me from home.

This old man, he play eight,
he play duck and obfuscate.
With a brainwrack, sidetrack,
who he is unknown,
this old man pretend he's home.

This old man, he play nine,
he play everything just fine.
With a handclap, laugh track,
telephone postpone,
this old man believes he's home.

This old man, he play ten,
he play Rex Coelestis, men.
With an ack-ack, nightflack,
flashbulb hecatomb,
this old man destroys our home.

Descending Moriah

On our way back down the mountain
my father walked beside me.
He did not look at me.
He spoke as if I had been spared.

On our way back down the mountain
a cascade roared in my head;
my legs would not stop shaking.
I did not recognize a single thing I saw.

I heard my mother call my name
and I hated the sound of her voice
and refused to answer.

On our way back down the mountain
I saw, already, in the torn morning,
the endless future of sons and bloodshed
and prayed I would go blind.

Materfamilias

Look, Ikey. Isaac. He didn't mean
no harm. For God's sake,
he's your father! He made you
that flute. Those are his sheep.
I know you need a little time.
But what about your father?
He feels terrible. And me.
Do you ever think about me?
We need things back to normal.
Come. Sit at the table. Eat.

Suite: In Lieu of a Legacy

I lived in one of the great cities
along a river spanned by beautiful bridges.
Trains ran overhead and underground.
Bells rang as if we were still in the old world,
trolleys passed, shopkeepers swept the sidewalks
or cranked down canvas awnings as before the war.
Every few moments a jet lifted off from the airport.

Everyone talked about money, having it or not.
We watched what everyone else was watching,
heard what everyone else was hearing, read
what everyone else was reading. Endless
arguments sought by disputation to discover
why so many women were dying and so many men
were empty of feeling except for a murderous rage.

And because, before I arrived here, I had lived
in another city of slow rivers and boulevards,
downtown bright with color for the holidays, music
and monuments, factories, ballfields, railroads, schools,
all gone now — not transformed, collapsed — I wonder,
walking the avenue eating ice cream, looking
in the windows at the new merchandise, how long
before the money finds its interest elsewhere,
leaving behind it video training games for the poor,
push-button killers on the sofa, slapping high fives,
knocking back shots in front of virtual tortures,
or stoned in front of wide-screen horror DVDs.

You have a right to ask why I am telling you this
in the past tense, clearly addressed to you in the future.
You have a right to ask if I tried to awaken,
or if I was among those paid to devise new ways
to remain asleep, or if I remained asleep myself.
(I am not sure, today, how I would answer.)
You have a right, like Dante, to condemn me
to the vestibule of hell where, neither in nor out,
I will prevaricate forever, comfortless, deliberating

whether to suck my left thumb or my right,
whether to stand or kneel, speak or remain silent,
and you have the right to refuse us all forgiveness.
I acknowledge it here and now. And yet I hope
what will come is no kingdom, no dominion,
no chink of coins, no rustle of bills; instead,
as before the long nightmare, the learning of poems,
the making of music, the trading of songs.

2.

I'm a son-of-a-gun.
I know, I know:

go ahead and groan
but it's more than a pun.

(If men shot arrows,
I'd be a bow's.)

A man shot his gun
at another and missed,

and went down, done
DNA in the dust.

The other went further,
became my father.

3.

uninformed
in uniform

formidable
disabled

bled
dis

4.

What was taken from me was taken from so many
everyone turns away or sneers if you bring it up.
I would have had enough of history too,
had I come home like my father (in one piece, yes,
but how many pieces had he been before?)
talking about having a roof over your head
you keep down, never volunteer, and mind
your business, get yours, war behind; but
then my uncle's war, all pictures of mud and rain
as if it had been some natural disaster; and then
my neighbors, friends' big brothers, off to the islands;
when they called my number, I said no and found
a shrink who for a couple hundred dollars
called me crazy; what I was was empty, the way
you're empty when you first wake up, alert, and listen
for something you thought you heard, a cry, maybe,
or a siren, but then you're not sure if it was a dream.
The news comes on and sets me straight: no dream.

5.

He still can't talk about it,
my father. A killer? But he is here
in the photo, rocking my child!

An infant crying in the crook
of practical tenderness, caught
with a fan-toed tiny foot stuck
out from the blanket, forever,

nothing of who he's become,
lifting me off the ground and
kissing me when he sees me now.

(He will mourn me one day, I hope,
and not the other way round.)

And his grandfather, captured here,
bows his head, purses his lips, and
gazes in incorruptible wonder.

6.

Aeneas, aged father on his back,
is framed in a falling doorway,
child by the hand, fire all around,
three generations of refugees,

home not the ashes behind them,
nor even the old address, but
a new place they yearn for:
kitchen, burial plot, and playground.

7.

The tale of our fathers'
grief, of their labor's
theft and our betrayal,

must now be told:
torn from our mothers,
told over and over

life is a bloodless secret
men share with the dead
and the love we thought

was ours for nothing
was nothing, we were led
in uniforms to stadiums

and called to prove
in blood we were not
what they called us

then, not then, not ever.
Now the stone breasts
of statues move us,

women with wings
not tears, and not these
hurt and angry mothers

of our sons and daughters
whose fears we no longer
remember, like peace.

8.

I prefer to think of him as an infant trying to learn
to bring his palms together, not a man with an injury

deep in his head, an obstacle of scar where a word,
the one he cannot find, is lodged, a pellet of shrapnel.

It is not that he cannot find things to applaud
but that he can no longer do so in the usual way

and has had to forget so much lest he come
to the end too soon, with nothing to desire.

9.

an infantryman,
a trying man, an
infant who can
think not one word,

an unman, an
obstacle, an end,
a scar, a future
he cannot find

10.

I wanted an explanation
too, but no one had one for me,
so I made one up. You want to hear it?
I didn't think so. What good
would it be to you? By the time enough
of what has happened in my time
is recognized in yours, it will be too late
and it will all be happening again.
That was, in fact, a part of my explanation.

11.

Ares, in a hurry always, in a moment before the meeting,
          takes Aphrodite from behind,
                    while Hades, already arrived,

runs the numbers one more time. The deal's
          already made — some gifts and a shake across mahogany
                    and they're out of there,

leaving by separate exits. No, no photographs, no paper,
          no record, though between them there are promises,
                    a contract, sure as a contract

for so many barrels of oil, so many miles of pipeline,
          a deal for so many souls has been brokered by men,
                    a deal for a number of souls

to be shrunk each to a drop of black blood and stored,
          bitter with remorse, with understanding come too late,
                    with longing for old enchantments,

in the many-chambered cellar of the pomegranate
          where, wine of recombinant myth, they wait,
                    aging in the bottle,

dark as ink, as the dark the new stories about them
        will claim to come from, as the dark of a theater
                        where our children, in rows,

thirsty, imbibe black promises, false premises,
        seeds of the pomegranate, mix of blood and oil,
                        another shipment of souls

warehoused and up for bid. What good has ever come
        of any kind of congress between the gods and men? Listen:
                        that is wailing you hear.

12.

An age ago. The names are changed,
and we are from new and different countries;
our tongues cannot make certain sounds
when we happen upon old tales in books,

though glyphs depict there people dancing,
rituals, records of conquest, feats of heroes,
fantastic animals in symbolic postures,
and naked slaves in familiar ones.

13.

You say history; I say robbery.
You say desire; I say necessity.

You answer God.
That wasn't what I asked.

Let us at least be honest.
Let us honor the dead.
Let us pray:

I want to be felled and burned.
I pray to be taken and used.
May I be chosen and consumed,
but let me say when and by whom.

Coda

What might he follow
to find his way home?

The need for his mother.
The grief in his father's eyes.

How will he know
he is nearing the place?

The way the sky
betrays the ocean,
the air the field of rye,
the cascade the unseen lake

higher in the mountains.

Acknowledgments

The author wishes to thank the editors of magazines in which some of the poems in this book have appeared, sometimes in slightly different versions:

"Gold Star Road," "Pantoum: But You Are Gone," "Déjà Vu" — *Agni*

"Summer Job," "Blog Pix: Fallujah," "Woodcut Parable, 15th C." — *Barrow Street*

"Vocation" — *Cedar Hill Review*

"An Emblem from Dresden," "Here Goes," "December," "Humility," "A Unit Deploys," and "Vanitas" — *Janus Head: Journal of Interdisciplinary Studies in Literature, Continental Philosophy, Phenomenological Psychology & the Arts*

"Refugee," "Suite: In Lieu of a Legacy" — *The Literary Review*

"Founders' Gallery," "Gift" — *Painted Bride Quarterly*

"Bosnia Aftermath" — *Poetry*

"Ars" — *Review Americana*

Poems on the World Wide Web:

"Broadcast," "The Judgment of Paris" — *Poets Against the War*

"Refugee" — *Verse Daily*

I would also like to thank Kathleen Aguero, Kurt Brown, Celia Gilbert, Jeffrey Harrison, Barbara Helfgott-Hyett, Linda McCarriston, Michael Morse, Dennis Nurkse, Saul Touster, Afaa Michael Weaver, and Baron Wormser: your expert advice suffuses these poems.

I am grateful to David Rosner and Ellen Schutz for their hospitality and generosity; likewise, B. Lee Hope and Bill Betcher.

I wish to thank Ellen, Mike, Mikele, Thom, Steve, and Zoya, the "soup group," for the privilege and blessing of your company.

My gratitude also to Barrow Street Press, especially my fine editors Peter Covino and Sarah Hannah.